بسم الله الرحمن الرحيم

A Blessed Olive Tree

A Spiritual Journey in Twenty Short Stories

Zain Hashmi

Illustrated by:	Riffat Ara Baig
Edited by:	Najam Hussain Tirmizi
Cover Artwork:	Muhammad Umair Chouhdry

To every living being, in this world and beyond.

CONTENTS

Acknowledgements

I would like to acknowledge these personalities for their inspiration while writing these short stories:

My ultimate inspiration is Prophet Muhammad ﷺ.

I received timeless inspiration from Abul Ala Maududi, Iqbal, Khwaja Ghulam Farid, Rumi, and Shah Hussain.

Living inspirations include Imran Khan, Liaqat Hashmi, Noman Ali Khan, Sheikh Hamza Yousaf, and Syed Maqbool Mohsin Gillani.

A Blessed Olive Tree

The War

The war began when our great-great grandfather[1] was forced to leave his home[2], and it will continue until we return and regain our place and honour.

Our King[3] is our Lord. We don't need to say "Long live the King"; He is immortal and so are we. We are here to fight, to win over the axis of evil, and return to our home, our paradise.

There are different groups of fighters. Most of them fight in the name of the King and in the command of our Great General[4]. Our General is also immortal, just like our King and like all of us, but he has returned. Returned to the King, but left behind the principles, timeless principles set forth in the Book of Wisdom[5]. There is no General after him. After him are only his deputies. We can all be his deputies.

No one has ever seen the King, but we all will one day. The King is very kind and loves His people. We all love Him and fight in His name, not for the reward of getting back to our home, or in fear of being thrown into the city of Hell.

Some of the fighters wear the best uniforms, do the best drills, but hardly anyone has seen them fighting. Some you won't even think that they are fighters, but they are the best knights on the battlefield. In the words of the Poet:

> *These warriors, they are your secretive men*
> *Whom you have granted the taste of divinity*[6]

Notes

1 Prophet Adam

2 Heaven

3 God

4 Prophet Muhammad ﷺ

5 The Quran

6 From "*Tariq ki Dua*" (Tariq's Prayer), an Urdu Poem by Iqbal.

Noor

A li opened his eyes and could not see anything, as it was pitch dark. He closed his eyes and opened them again, but the same darkness surrounded him. He tried again and again but couldn't see anything, even though his eyes were wide open.

He soon recalled that he was in a cave that had no light. He had ended up in that cave after following a band of bandits who used it to store their loot. He had followed them out of greed for gold and silver. He had always had a lust for gold and silver. Being a young boy, he envied people who were rich and wanted to be like them, or even richer. The idea of them being rich and him having merely enough sometimes stirred him up and had even landed him in fights with the wealthy boys in town.

He recalled that he had tried different ways to get rich quick, and had said bad things about people in front of their rivals to gain their rivals' confidence and learn their secrets. Then one day, he learned about a notorious band of bandits and heard stories of their great hoard of stolen treasure. He decided to find this band, follow it, and steal their treasure from them. Looting from the bandits did not seem to be a bad thing to him. "There should be nothing wrong with that," he thought. "After all, all that wealth doesn't belong to them, so if I take it, then I could keep it."

After searching for a long time, he somehow managed to find the bandits, follow them to their cave of loot, and secretly enter while they were sleeping. Ali finally saw all the gold and silver with his own eyes, of which he had only heard of until then. There were piles of gold and silver coins lying in the cave as if they were grain lying in the fields to dry. He was very happy to have found such wealth. It was like his dream had come true. He had already started to plan how he would spend this wealth when he returned to the town. Ali hid in a dark corner and waited for the bandits to wake up and leave so he could carry the gold and silver coins back to his home. While waiting and making plans about how to spend this wealth, he fell asleep.

He finally woke up and found the cave to be very dark. He could not see the opening of the cave, as it was closed, and it seemed that the bandits had left, since he couldn't hear anything. He carefully began to look for the opening of the cave. He could feel the gold and silver coins around him. He could touch them and hear them, but could not see them. He kept on trying to find the way out, but he couldn't. He had no idea where he had entered from. He remembered that there was a small opening on one side of the cave, but which side, he could not guess. He never really thought that it would get so dark inside. He hadn't tried to remember the way out, as if the cave would always be lit.

After trying to find the way out for a long while, Ali felt completely lost. He had lost all sense of direction. He did not know if it was day or night. He felt like a blind person, but even blind people would have been better off, as their other senses would have been sharper, but here he felt completely lost in the deep darkness. He tried to cheer himself up by thinking about the gold and silver coins, but he kept wishing that they were candles or lamps, or anything that he could use to find his way out.

Time passed by. With each passing second, he became sadder and weaker. He now felt that he was going to die in that cave of hunger and thirst, or that the bandits would come back and kill him. He felt like he was buried alive. This idea made him even more sad and low. He remembered his mother and father, who were no longer alive. He remembered how his mother had wanted him to study hard and be a noble person, but he had not listened to her. He had stayed in the company of bad friends and left school. Instead of being noble, he had spent his days in the streets, calling other boys names, making fun of the elderly, stealing things from the shopkeepers, and teasing women in the bazaars. He saw his past as it flashed through his mind, and now he found himself dying in this deep, dark hole with all this gold and silver around him, but of no use to him. Lost in all these thoughts, he fell asleep once more.

He awoke once again. He felt weak with hunger and thirst. As he recalled how he had ended up there, all the negative thoughts returned. He then remembered his mother. He remembered her saying that if you regret something, then promise yourself never to do it again, and if you regret not doing something, then promise yourself to do it no matter how late it is. And never forget the promises you make to yourself.

He promised in his heart that if he ended up coming out of this cave, he would do as his mother told him to, and would quit all the bad habits that had led him to this misery. He also remembered his father, who used to say that one should never, ever give up. Remembering this lifted him a bit, and he decided to search for the way out one more time. He stood up and started walking slowly by moving his hands along the walls of the cave to find an opening. He walked through the gold and silver coins as if they were not even grain, but perhaps just some pebbles.

He kept on moving. This time, he was trying harder not to miss even an inch along the wall that might lead to some way out. Suddenly, he found a very small hole in the wall. He could hardly put his finger through it, but he found that it was soft around the edges. He started scratching at the edges to make the hole bigger, and was very excited to discover that it was widening. He then started using both his hands to make it bigger and bigger. The hope of escaping the cave filled him with energy. He kept on digging the hole, and had finally made it big enough to pass through. He could not see any light on the other side, but he was hopeful that there must be some way out.

Ali crawled through the hole and entered a chamber that was dark, but he had a feeling that it wasn't as dark as the first cave. He felt that there was a light somewhere nearby, so he kept on moving carefully, checking the walls with his hands, in the direction he thought the light might be. His hands finally found a niche in the wall... the kind of niche that is made to hold lamps. He became very excited and thought he might find a magic lamp. Before, he had been looking for light, but now he was expecting something even better; not just a lamp, but a magic lamp.

As his hands were trying to find the lamp in the niche in the dark, they touched something that was definitely a lamp, but it wasn't the kind of lamp that he was expecting. It was an old upright lamp with a glass covering. The glass seemed to be covered with dark filth that made it impossible for any light to escape, had it been lit. Ali harboured the hope that there might be a flame in that lamp that the filthy glass kept him from seeing. He tried to expose the light of the lamp by cleaning the glass with his sleeves, but he found that the dark filth was very hard, and couldn't be removed.

Once again, he began to lose hope. His hunger and thirst returned, and he felt that he was losing energy. He tried to collect his thoughts. He realized that when he had found the nook, the greed had taken hold of him again, and he had started to look for a magic lamp instead of an ordinary lamp that would simply show him a way out of this darkness. He realized that ever since his parents passed, he had spent his life doing things that they had always forbidden, and hadn't done what they had wanted him to. He had ended up in the cave because of his bad habits, and his heart was still following greed.

He repented that very moment and made a promise in his heart that if he made it out of this cave, he wouldn't fall victim to greed, envy, anger, backbiting, stealing, disrespect, teasing, or idleness ever again, and would live his life the way his parents had wanted him to. He remembered his mother and father, and as he did, tears poured from his eyes and fell on the glass of the lamp.

He was surprised to see that his tears had washed all the filth off the glass, which became crystal-clear and twinkled like a white star. To his amazement, as soon as the glass was clean and gleaming, he saw a tiny flame in the lamp, but it looked as if it was about to die. It gave off very little light – not enough to light up its surroundings. Ali was happy to find the flame, but was also worried, as he did not want this flame to die. It looked like there wasn't enough oil in the lamp to fuel the flame. He looked closely at the lamp and found an inscription around the flame that read:

"Lit from [the oil of] a blessed olive tree,
Neither of the East nor of the West"

He took the lamp and started to look around, hoping that the flame would stay alive long enough for him to find some oil. There wasn't much in that part of the chamber, so he decided to go back to the other side where all the gold and silver coins were. He crawled back to the other side while carefully holding the lamp with both hands.

The first cave was filled with gold and silver, but there was no oil. He searched every corner, but it was no use. He prayed that he would find oil for the lamp before the flame died. "Why not find my way out with whatever flame the lamp still had?" he thought. But the cave was huge, and the lamp had very little light. That tiny flame could hardly help him see a few inches.

Disappointment came over him once again. He started to lose hope. He remembered his mother again, and recalled how good she was, how concerned she was for his well-being. He regretted that he had never loved his mother as he should have loved her. He never praised her as he should have praised her. He remembered how loving his father was, how he wanted his son to be like him: successful, respectful, and noble. But he had forgotten all his parents' teachings, and behaved with complete ignorance after their passing.

He recalled that his mother had a book that she called the Book of Wisdom, and that she had told him to always refer to that book whenever he did not know what to do. He wished that he had that book with him so he could read it; even though his parents were not with him, at least he would still have that book.

"But here in this dark cave," he thought, "how can I find that book... Book? Why I am thinking of a book? I was looking for oil... Oil? Why should I be looking for oil? I should be looking for the way out of this cave... Way out? Oil? Book... Book... Oil... Way out..."

He fell unconscious.

Ali opened his eyes and then closed them again quickly, as the cave was filled with light. He slowly opened his eyes once more, and found that the lamp burned with a strong flame, as if it were fueled by some very special oil. The glass around the flame was sparkling, which made the light spread even further across the cave. The whole cave was illuminated, completely flooded with light. The heaps of gold and silver coins were still there, glittering in the light, but for some reason, Ali was not attracted to that glitter. That gold and silver had not helped him when he was in need. He was more amazed and mesmerized by the light of the lamp, so strong and so beautiful. He took the lamp, and its pure and beautiful light soon helped him find the way out.

Before leaving the cave, he gazed at the gold and silver for the last time, but he remembered the promises he had made to himself. He did not feel any attraction to the treasure, as he knew that it did not belong to him and so he should not take it. He was taking a much more valuable thing from there: the lamp whose light could help him find all the ways to success. He held the lamp and walked straight out of the cave.

Ali returned to his home, and the first thing he did was find the Book of Wisdom. It was wrapped in a fancy cloth, yet was covered with dust. He brushed away the dust, unwrapped the book, and then his eyes filled with tears as he remembered his mother and father. They had left this beautiful gift for him but he had never even looked at it. As he opened the book, he felt as if he wasn't an orphan any more, and that his parents were still with him. He started to read the book. He reached the Chapter of Light, and the thirty-fifth verse read:

"Allah is the Light of the heavens and the earth. The example of His light is like a niche within which is a lamp, the lamp is within glass, the glass as if it were a pearly [white] star lit from [the oil of] a blessed olive tree, neither of the east nor of the west, whose oil would almost glow even if untouched by fire. Light upon light. Allah guides to His light whom He wills. And Allah presents examples for the people, and Allah is Knowing of all things."

He looked in the mirror. He saw himself, and how his chest looked like the niche. Within it, he saw his heart illuminated as a lamp. His strong character surrounded the lamp like a sparkling glass, protecting the flame and increasing the light of his heart. He promised himself that he would never let his deeds darken the clear glass of his character again. His soul was the flame Allah put in him when he and everyone else was created, and this flame must be fed with the oil of the blessed olive tree, the divine guidance in the Book of Wisdom (the Quran) and the teachings of the Holy Prophet ﷺ.

And when your soul, the flame, the spark, meets with the divine fuel that is so pure and so strong, it results in immense enlightenment: the enlightenment of God. Light upon light. *Noorun Alaa Noor.*

Return

Saalihah[1] opened her eyes. She was in a hospital bed, and felt weak. This sickness was getting worse with each passing day, but she hoped to see Ameer before she died. The war was almost over, and most of the men had returned to their homes, but Ameer was not back yet. Every day, she waited for him in the hope of seeing him again one more time. The wait was even more painful than her sickness. She knew that every person had to die someday. She was ready for that, but Ameer... he should have returned by now. He belonged to her. He had promised her that he would be with her in health and sickness. She understood that his duty to his country was more important, but the war was over now. "Where is he? Why has he not returned to me?"

This war had been on since she was a child, with few interludes, but hopefully it would truly be finished now. She remembered when, as a child, she had been sent to a boarding school[2] for a short time because of the war. She had never wanted to leave her parents, her house, or her town, but all the kids were being sent to smaller towns. While she was at the boarding school, she knew that it was only temporary. Once things returned to normal, she would be sent back to her home. Her new school was nestled up in the mountains, a beautiful location with wonderful scenery, but she knew in her heart that she did not belong in that place. It was a short-term arrangement, and she would leave as soon as things got better in her hometown[3].

Her parents told her to do her best, stay at the top, and prove herself in her new school. She asked her parents why she needed to do well, since she wasn't going to stay in that school forever. Her father told her, "It does not matter if you are in a school for a day or for a decade. You should do your best. Be a role model for others. Everyone should be proud of you, and besides, your future depends on your performance there. You could be admitted to the best school in town on your return if you perform well, or end up going to the worst one if you don't." She listened to her father and followed his teachings.

The boarding school was really nice, with a beautiful building, lush, green lawns, and colourful flowers with butterflies flying over them, but despite all this, her heart always yearned for the place where she belonged... her hometown, her house, her parents.

* * * * *

It now seemed like she had lived her life, and that death was not far away, but Ameer... he should have returned. She said to herself, "He belonged to me. When I was at the boarding school, I even kept my little watch set to the same time as my hometown. I never changed it to the time of that beautiful town in the hills. Most of the girls used to think that my watch kept the wrong time.

Little did they know that it was the *right* time. It was the time in my hometown, the place where I belong. Where I grew up, where my house was, where my parents lived. How could that be wrong? For me, that was the right time.

"Ameer must have remembered me. He couldn't have forgotten me. I know he went to war... wars are bloody and wars are cruel, but not cruel enough to make someone forget where they belong. He couldn't have forgotten me or his home. He will return... he will return soon."

Death seemed to be imminent now. She remembered how once when she was a child, she had gone to a graveyard with her mother. Seeing some of the ancient graves there, she had asked her mother, "If it's true that all the dead will be brought to life again, how could the people in these old graves be brought back to life?"

Her mother had replied, "Saalihah, do you see those grassy plains? See how green they are. They were not like that for years because of the drought. It was barren land, but once it rained, the grass grew again. Do you know why?"

"Why?" Saalihah had asked.

"Because the seed of that grass never died. It remained alive underneath the soil, and when it rained, the grass grew again."

"Do us humans have seeds?" asked Saalihah.

"Yes, my dear, we do have seeds, or cells, or something, which doesn't die if it's buried for years, or submerged under water, or even if it gets burned. All humans will be brought to life just as the grass comes to life again after years of drought.[4]"

"Where will we go once we are brought back to life?" asked Saalihah.

"The good belong in heaven, and they will live there happily ever after".

"You mean they won't die again?"

"No, they won't," her mother had replied.

"So that means that humans are immortals!" said Saalihah, and her mother had smiled and nodded.

* * * * *

"I am not afraid of death, but all I want is to see Ameer for one last time before I die. He must have returned by now." Saalihah felt weak, and closed her eyes.

She opened her eyes slowly, and could not believe it! It was Ameer, dressed in his uniform, standing by her side, holding her hand. Saalihah smiled and said, "Thank God! Ameer, you've finally returned!"

Ameer smiled back and replied. "My love, look around you. It's not me... it is *you* who has returned."

18

Notes

¹ "Pious and righteous"

² This world

³ Heaven

⁴ Grass growing on barren land after rain refers to men and women being brought back to life after death, as mentioned in (Q41:39):

> *"And of His signs is that you see the earth submissive. Then when We send down water upon it, it shakes and swells. Surely He Who gives life to it is indeed He Who gives life to the dead; surely He is Ever-Determiner over everything."*

and in (Q22:5):

> *"O People, if you should be in doubt about the Resurrection, then [consider that] indeed, We created you from dust, then from a sperm-drop, then from a clinging clot, and then from a lump of flesh, formed and unformed - that We may show you. And We settle in the wombs whom We will for a specified term, then We bring you out as a child, and then [We develop you] that you may reach your [time of] maturity. And among you is he who is taken in [early] death, and among you is he who is returned to the most decrepit [old] age so that he knows, after [once having] knowledge, nothing. And you see the earth barren, but when We send down upon it rain, it quivers and swells and grows [something] of every beautiful kind."*

The Orange Tree

"So here is your orange tree[1], Sir. It's all yours. Enjoy its fresh oranges, beautiful orange flowers, and heavenly scent."

"Thank you very much," said Omer. "I will take good care of it. I would appreciate it if you could give me some care advice for it."

"Sure, no problem. Just follow these five easy procedures[2], and your plant will stay in great shape. First, if possible and feasible, bring it to our farm once, only once in your lifetime, whenever you think you can[3]. It would be great if you could. At the farm, it will be kind of overhauled and will get a new life."

"And what if I am not able to?" asked Omer.

"No problem, Sir. If you aren't able to, then there is no compulsion."

"Second, for one month each year, don't water it or feed it any fertilizer when the sun is up[4]. You can feed and water it at night, but not while the sun is up, irrespective of whether it's spring or fall."

"Won't that hurt the poor plant?" asked Omer. "It could dehydrate it in the summers or could also hurt during the winters."

"No, Sir, it won't. Don't you worry, it will actually be very healthy for your orange tree. You will notice the difference. It will help balance out any extra intake, make it tough to bear all conditions, and will put your plant in alignment with the other ones that originated from the same farm."

"What if the plant is in really bad shape, and can't afford to be without water or food?" asked Omer.

"Well, there are exceptions. This procedure is not meant to hurt the plant, but actually to help nourish it."

"Oh, okay, that's a relief."

"Third, you have to trim it every year[5]. Once a year is fine. Get rid of the extra branches and leaves."

"Won't that hurt it or slow down its growth, or even hurt its production?" Omer asked.

"No, Sir. Actually, it will do the opposite. The trimming will increase the flowers, scent, and ultimately the fruit."

"So far, all the care procedures have been yearly affairs, but now here is something you need to do every day. You have to change the sides of the plant to make sure it gets maximum sunshine and fresh air[6]. First early in the morning before the sunrise, then right after midday, then in the late afternoon, then as soon as the sun goes down, and finally when it's completely dark."

"Flipping sides again and again… Well, that is something that needs persistence. Is there any relaxation to this procedure?" asked Omer.

"No, Sir. Sorry, the moving is mandatory. While there is some relaxation if you are travelling or are unable to do it, it is beneficial for your plant, and will keep it healthy and free of any diseases, viruses, and pests."

"Oh, okay. And what if I miss some or all of these care measures?" asked Omer.

"Some people knowingly or unknowingly end up doing that, but they are left with their orange tree in bad shape. Their tree does not produce any fruit, flowers, or even scent."

"Don't they die?" asked Omer.

"No. No, Sir, they don't. They are not meant to die. They can be in very bad shape, but they live no matter how poorly their keepers keep them."

"Does anything else need to be taken care of?" asked Omer.

"Yes, Sir. Last but not least, always use the same sod for your orange tree[7]. The same that it had at our main farm. You can find it easily all across, so always use that. Do not use any other sod, or the tree will be ruined. These are the tree's basic care procedures. You can do more if you wish."

"Any other tips for me?" asked Omer.

"Other than care, Sir? My personal advice: try to share its fruit with as many people as you can, and also make sure that no one is ever hurt by your orange tree."

"How long do they live?" asked Omer.

"Sir don't worry about their life… they last a lifetime."

"Yes, but from what I understand, it will need to be returned to the main farm when I don't need it anymore."

"Sir, please allow me to correct you. Actually, the orange tree will need to be returned when it won't need *you*."

"It won't need me? Sorry, I don't get it," said Omer.

"Sir, I am sorry to say that you won't be around to be of any help."

"Where will I be?" asked Omer.

"Oh, Sir! Did I forget to mention that? By then, you will actually *become* your orange tree!"

Notes

---

[1] The human spirit. The soul.

[2] The five pillars of Islam.

[3] The fifth and final pillar of Islam: *Hajj*, the pilgrimage.

[4] The fourth pillar of Islam: *Saum*, fasting.

[5] The third pillar of Islam: *Zakat*, obligatory charity.

[6] The second pillar of Islam: *Salat*, praying.

[7] First Pillar of Islam: *Shahada*, saying and believing that there is no God but Allah, and that Muhammad ﷺ is the messenger of Allah.

Kumari

"Kumari, you are the love of my life," said Momin. "I cannot think of living without you. I want to marry you, but the only hurdle is the difference in our faiths. Kumari… please convert so we can marry."

"Why do I need to convert?" Kumari asked.

"Because you are a Hindu and I am a Muslim, "Momin replied. "You have to become a Muslim so we can marry."

"And how do I become a Muslim?" Kumari asked.

"Oh, all you need to do is say the Shahada. It's simple."

"Really? That seems easy. What is the Shahada?" asked Kumari.

"The Shahada is basically saying that there is no God but Allah…"

"You mean Ishwar," Kumari interrupted.

"Yes, but we call him Allah."

"But how come one becomes Muslim just by saying the Shahada?" asked Kumari.

"I'm not done yet, Kumari! 'There is no God but Allah, and Muhammad is the messenger of God'."

"Okay, are you done now?" asked Kumari.

"Yes, I am," Momin replied.

"Okay, how can one become a Muslim just by saying it? Don't you have to believe it as well?"

"Isn't that the same thing?" asked Momin.

"No, Momin, it's not the same thing. A person can say something without knowing exactly what it means, and without believing in it. And another person might believe in something without saying anything."

"What do you mean?" asked Momin.

"Do you believe in the Shahada?" Kumari asked.

"I am a *born* Muslim. What are you talking about?"

"No, answer me… do you believe in the Shahada?"

"Yes, I do. There is no question about it."

"Okay. You say that you believe in the Shahada, which means that you believe in one God."

"Yes, one God. Not like the thousands of gods and goddesses in your religion."

"But I have not seen you praying to that one God."

"Well, yes, I don't pray… most Muslims are like that, but that doesn't mean that I don't believe in one God," replied Momin.

"Sorry, Momin. I've never seen you praying, and that's what made me suspicious. I've never seen you fasting or doing any act of worship."

"You don't have to worship, and especially not in public…"

"Do you worship in private?"

"Well, you don't *have* to worship to prove your belief."

"Then how *do* you?" asked Kumari.

"I have believed in one God since I was born. I was given Azan in my ear on the day I was born, I was circumcised…"

"Momin, I am simply asking how you would prove that you believe in one God."

"Are you questioning my faith?"

"If you are not doing what God or your Allah has asked you to do, then it is getting a little difficult for me to see how you truly believe in that God. I think you *think* that you believe, but…"

29

"But what, you think I am an infidel like you?"

"I believe in Ishwar, one God. I pray to Him."

"Yes, you pray, but in front of idols."

"But at least I pray."

"But you don't believe in the Prophet, Kumari."

"You mean in Muhammad Sahib," Kumari said respectfully.

"Yes, in *Prophet* Muhammad," Momin corrected.

"And what exactly do I have to believe?" asked Kumari.

"That he is the messenger of God," replied Momin.

"Do you believe in him?" asked Kumari.

"Yes, of course I do! I am a Muslim."

"Why do you think that you have to be Muslim to believe in him? Isn't he mentioned as 'Mercy for all the worlds.' in your Quran?"

"Kumari, don't try to teach me my own religion. All I am asking is… are you willing to convert?"

"Convert to what?"

"Convert to Muslim, for God's sake!"

"Momin…, I think *you* should convert."

"What?! You want me to become a Hindu?" asked Momin.

"No, Momin, I want you to become a Muslim… a true Muslim."

Success

Hassan was compiling his notes for his presentation, "Success". He interviewed people from different backgrounds, professions, and trades. All he wanted to make sure of was that the people who were giving their views should at least be somewhat successful in their own lives, and that their views were based on their own personal experiences. Their opinions were as different as the people themselves. Some were quite interesting, like:

"Everyone should do some exercise every day to stay fit and healthy. Nothing intense, just something light. Yoga is a great exercise. You can do it without any weights or equipment. You can do it anywhere. It keeps you active and healthy, prevents back pain, sciatica, etc. You feel good after doing it. It requires consistency. Once you start doing it and form a habit, then you won't want to miss it. It will refresh you. Refresh your body, and even soul. Your thought process becomes smoother. Your brain gets more oxygen. You feel light. You feel great. You feel successful.[1]"

"Discipline in life is very important. We need to divide our time into productive time frames. Life should be more structured.

Time management is very important. Once time is divided into different time frames, then productivity can be enhanced. I think this is very important for success. ²"

"Hygiene is very important. These days, there are all sorts of diseases spreading from one person to another. Everyone should be very careful about this. The best prevention is washing your hands more often. Keep yourself clean. Avoid germs and diseases. You will be successful if you are healthy. Health is wealth, health is success. ³"

"We are moving away from nature. Our life has become very artificial. Now we don't know when the sun rises or when it sets. We follow watches, not nature. We should be more aware of our surroundings, as it used to be for centuries. We should know when the sun is rising, when it is moving towards the horizon, when it sets, when weather changes. When the moon rises, and when the stars shine. For me, real success isn't which latest gadget you are using, but rather how close you are with nature and its system. ⁴"

"I don't like to please the people I don't like. I don't like them, not because of anything else, but because they don't do things right, and then they want me to appreciate their not doing right. No, I can't do that. Please don't ask me to do it. It's not ego, it's who I am. This is my programming. This is how I should be. This is how everyone should be. You may think I am wrong, but please don't ask me to not do what I do. Well, success, short term it may seem like you won't get it if you are like me, but I bet you that to be a real success, this is very important.[5]"

"Start right. If you keep doing what was started right, it will result in a right ending. So always start right, and you will be successful.[6]"

"Always be thankful of whatever you have. Try for better, but remain thankful. You will be very successful.[7]"

"Appreciate kindness and gentleness. It will help you and people around you become kind and gentle, which will result in less friction and resistance towards success.[8]"

"We should not consider success a short term, visible thing. It could be very different than what it looks like. You must have a strong belief that your life will not end with death. You are immortal. You were always there and you always will be. Your next life is based on your actions in this life, which is much shorter compared to the life in the next world. Short-term successes (of this world) may be a problem for the long-term success of the next world if those successes are achieved by wrongdoing. Focus on overall success in this world and the next. A win-win situation. Not a win for you for the price of loss for others. Real success is sharing the success.[9]"

"Success for me is… you know the old saying, balancing four things: career, health, family, and spirituality. These days, we somehow manage the first three, but we don't have time for the fourth one. Everyone is busy... who cares about spirituality? But let me tell you, it is very important. Your mind needs to be connected to some force, some divine presence, whatever you call it. It will fuel you, your dreams, and your passion. Give you confidence, contentment, a secure feeling. A feeling of being watched over, being taken care of, being looked after. A feeling that you are not alone, there is a divine presence by your side in everything you do, in everything you plan. It gives you a great power, and in my opinion, that is really what you need to be successful.[10]"

"If you are constantly – I will say again – constantly looking to improve yourself, trying to be better, and open to change for betterment, it's not the case that you will eventually become successful. I would say you are *already* successful. Making the right choices, no matter how small they are, is so important. Small good decisions will lead you to the glorious path of success.[11]"

"Just follow the successful and don't follow the unsuccessful. It's very simple: you will become successful by following successful people.[12]"

"Don't be lost. Have an opinion, have a say, but don't be lost ever. That's the worst you could ever wish for. If you are not lost, then you will be on the right track, because most of the people who are on the wrong one actually think that they are lost. No one willingly chooses the wrong path.[13]"

"Find a success mentor, a coach. It helps in all fields of life, and it also helps in becoming successful.[14]"

"If you consider yourself among the top, you will automatically become tuned to do as they do or have done. It's not about raising your ego or arrogance. It's about raising your character. It's about raising your value, yourself. Once you believe you are among the best, you will do as the best do and the result is obvious... success.[15]"

"Be a believer. Have faith and have conviction. If you have this, success will be yours.[16]"

"Think collectively. Open your horizons. Think of others and others will think of you. Associate yourself with a larger group, family, society, or whatever you think your mind is capable of.[17]"

"Consistency is the key. Whatever you do, do it with consistency, and success will be yours.[18]"

"Do what you would like your children to do. Everyone loves their family and thinks best for their children. If you do what you want your kids to be doing, you will be successful.[19]"

"Ask. Always ask. Don't be shy. To complete a sale, you need to ask the customer. To marry, you need to ask the girl. To know, you need to ask. To have something, you need to ask, and most likely you will get what you ask for.[20]"

"Don't do anything if you think you are going to regret it. Think twice. If there is even a slim possibility that you will regret doing something, don't do it. If you end up doing something regretful, never do it again, but it's better to avoid it in the first place. Follow this rule and success will be yours.[21]"

Hassan thought, "Wow, what great ideas! I think I have enough material for my presentation".

The call for prayer was given nearby. The following words struck him: *"Come to success... Come to success"*. He thought of saying his prayer, which he hadn't done in a long while, and when he did, he was surprised to realize that all his notes on success were to be found in what he did or said in that five-minute prayer.

Notes

[1] The Prayer (*Salat*) itself, which is performed five times a day.

[2] Intervals between each mandatory prayer.

[3] Ablution (*Wadu*), which is a prerequisite of prayer (*Salat*).

[4] The way prayer timings are based on nature, like sunrise, its movement, and sunset (and are not based on time).

[5] Not pleasing or rather worshipping humans, but the creator of humans. In the beginning of the prayer the following is read:

"Glory be to You, O Allah, and all praises are due unto You, and blessed is Your name and high is Your majesty, and none is worthy of worship but You."

[6] Refers to the first verse of the first chapter of Quran, which is read in all prayers:

"In the name of Allah, the all merciful, the ever merciful." (Q1:1)

[7] *"Praise be to Allah, the lord of the worlds." (Q1:2)* This is read to praise and thank the lord.

[8] *"The all merciful, the ever merciful." (Q1:3)*

[9] *"Master of the day of Judgement." (Q1:4)*

[10] *"You only do we worship and you only do we ask for help." (Q1:5)*

[11] *"Show us the straight path." (Q1:6)*

[12] *"The path of those whom you have blessed, who have not deserved your wrath…." (in Q1:7)*

[13] *"…nor gone astray." (in Q1:7)*

[14] *"Peace be upon you, O Prophet, and Allah's mercy and blessings be on you."* This is also read in the prayer.

[15] *"Peace be on us and on all righteous slaves of Allah."* This is read in the prayer.

[16] *"I bear witness that no one is worthy of worship except Allah and I bear witness that Muhammad is His slave and Messenger."* This is also read in the prayer.

[17] Refers to a prayer for the Prophet 🕌, his family, and all believers, and is read in the prayer (*Salat*) as follows:

> *"Oh Allah, send grace and honour on Muhammad and on the family and true followers of Muhammad just as you sent Grace and Honour on Ibrahim and on the family and true followers of Ibrahim. Surely, you are praiseworthy, the Great. Oh Allah, send your blessings on Muhammad and on the family and the true followers of Muhammad, just as you sent blessings on Ibrahim and the family and his true followers. Surely, you are Most Praiseworthy, the Exalted."*

[18] Refers to the beginning of (Q9:40), which is also read in the prayer:

> *"Lord! Make me one who keeps up the prayer …"*

[19] Refers to the middle of (Q9:40):

> *"…and of my offspring (ones who keep up the prayer)…"*

[20] Refers to the end of (Q9:40):

> *"….our Lord, and graciously accept my prayer."*

[21] Refers to (Q9:41):

> *"Our Lord, forgive me, and my parents, and the believers upon the Day when the reckoning will come up."*

Investment

"Giving away two-and-a-half percent of my excess funds and assets every year? Well, that's like a tax[1]. Even taxes ensure *some* benefits, but this is just paying for nothing, and is also mandatory. Wow, and then I am asked to pay *other* taxes as well, some of which are mandatory and others that are recommended!

"I have to pay off my mortgage, invest in my retirement savings, and then there is an education plan for my children, life insurance, and so on. Then on top of all *that* is this mandatory tax, and I'm warned that if I refuse to pay it, I'll be sent to Hell. I think this tax is like a bribe for not being sent to Hell!"

30 Years Later…

"Well, the mortgage is paid off. Now finally I own my house. I have enough in my retirement savings to last the rest of my life. My kids have completed their education. Their education plan was a blessing; they didn't have to take on any loans for their tuition fees. I have life insurance, too, so I am quite okay. But this two and half a percent every year… I never understood it. Why I am responsible for paying the poor? That should be the government or the NGOs' job. Why do I, as an individual, have a liability to pay this every year? I don't get it."

Ten Years Later…

"I don't see the house that I owned any more. I spent so many years paying off the mortgage for that house, but it's not there anymore. My retirement savings are also gone. Again, I saved money my whole life, but now it all seems to have disappeared. The kids' education savings has already been spent, and spent well. Life insurance? Oh, my family must have received it by now…

"What is this folder? Oh, it seems like I *was* able to bring some of my cash with me into this world… good to know! It's not the mortgage payments, and it's not any other savings, so what is it? It's the accumulated two and half percent and other "taxes" that I paid!

"Now I know. Back then, it was really hard to understand what I was paying for. I never knew that this would be the only monetary savings I could carry over to this world. I'm so glad I did pay that tax!"

Notes

---

[1] The third pillar of Islam, mandatory charity (*Zakat*).

Mother

"Raees, wake up. It's time for Sahoor. Wake up and eat."

"Mother, I don't want to fast. I won't be eating."

"Why aren't you fasting, son? Are you sick?"

"No, I'm not, but if I fast, I'll definitely get sick. It's too hot, and it's such a long day. I don't want to fast. I don't want to get sick."

"I haven't seen a single person get sick because of fasting in my whole life, but I *have* seen many people get sick by overeating. Come on, get up and eat. There isn't much time left."

"Mom, I have a busy schedule today. I'm not gonna sit idle all day just because I'm fasting."

"What sort of busy schedule do you have?"

"I have meetings and work to do… lots of brainwork."

"You will be doing it in the office, right?"

"Yes, of course… in the office."

"Your office is air-conditioned. And it's all 'brainwork', right? No physical work?"

"Yes, Mom. Of course there's no physical work, but brainwork also requires a lot of energy."

"Your father used to say that if you are busy doing brainwork while fasting, the time passes really quickly, and you don't really feel much hunger or thirst."

"Dad was different, Mom. In Ramadan, he also used to go to the gym just before Iftar... I can't do that!"

"What about more than fourteen hundred years ago in the desert of Arabia, when there was no air conditioning, no refrigerators, and not even electric fans? Most people used to do physical work, but they still fasted."

"Mom, please don't lecture me anymore! I really don't feel like fasting. Why are you trying to be cruel?"

"I'm not trying to be cruel... I'm actually trying to be kind. You won't be eating or drinking for the day, but your soul will be nourished during that time, and I also don't want my son to be in trouble in the next world. A little pain today will save you from much greater pain tomorrow."

"Mom, why do you think you have the right to impose your ideas on me? I am all grown up, I make my own living, live in my own apartment, and buy my own clothes. I'm not dependent on you at all, but you still treat me like I'm a 2-year-old and try to impose your will on me!"

"I am not imposing my will, dear. I'm just trying to help. I apologize if I have hurt you. By the way, yes, you're all grown up, you make your own living, live in your own apartment, and buy your own clothes, but under those clothes is a body that was once a part of me, and I still think it's no different than my own self… Bless you, my son."

House of God

Khalil went to his friend's house before leaving for the Pilgrimage to Makkah. He had heard that it's good to visit your friends and relatives before you start the holy journey. He reached Danish's place and told him that he was planning to go on the Pilgrimage.

Danish was delighted to hear his plans. He said, "You're lucky to be going at such a young age. Actually, everyone should go when they are young so they have the energy and health to carry out all the rituals, and also so that they are blessed early in their life."

Khalil said, "People have given me all kinds of advice. Is there something you would like to add?"

Danish said, "Well, you know what you need to do, but I would simply like to tell you the story of another friend who went on the pilgrimage. When he returned, he told us that during his pilgrimage, he lost a pair of slippers outside the gate of the Haram. He said that when he was praying for all manner of worldly things, it felt like he was praying for nothing more than the pair of slippers that he had lost at the gate."

"So what did he do then?" asked Khalil.

"He wasn't sure what he should pray for. He thought of everything he could possibly want and prayed for that, but still it seemed like it wasn't worth any more than a pair of slippers. He wasn't sure what to ask for or do. One night, after saying prayers in the Haram, he fell asleep for a while and had a dream.

"He saw himself all dressed up like a groom. His family was also very well-dressed. They were ready to go to his fiancée's house for his wedding. His fiancée, the love of his life, lived in another city. The plan was to go there, have lunch with her family, and bring her back so they could both live happily ever after. In the dream, he and his family drove for hours and finally reached at his fiancée's house. He rang the doorbell, but strangely, no one opened the door. He waited for a while tried again, but there was still no response. He got worried, and pushed on the door. To his relief, it opened, and he walked inside.

"The entire house was beautifully decorated. He entered the dining room; the lunch was all prepared, but there was no sign of the hosts. Everyone was astonished, but they didn't have any choice but to sit and wait. He waited anxiously for his fiancée and her family, but no one showed up. Someone suggested that since the food was all ready, why not have lunch while they waited? Hesitantly, everyone agreed, and they all enjoyed a warm and delicious lunch. After having lunch, he felt a little embarrassed, as he was there to take his fiancée as his bride, not to eat lunch.

"There was still no sign of the hosts. He looked around the house a few times, but couldn't find anyone. By then, his family members wanted to leave, as they had planned to be home by nightfall. They all began to ask him to leave with them, but he wasn't prepared to go back without his bride, the love of his life. His family kept trying to convince him to go, but he wouldn't leave without her. As he dreamed of this miserable situation, he heard the sound of Azan, and woke up.

"After saying his prayers, he thought about the dream and he realized that the house of his fiancée in the dream was actually the house of God. 'I was having a delicious, warm lunch at my fiancée's house, which I could have had anywhere else, just like I am praying for all these worldly things in the house of God, which I could pray for anywhere. In the dream, I was at my fiancée's house for *her*, to see her, to take her along with me so she could live with me forever, and here I am at God's house. I should pray for Him, for God to be the mate of my house, my heart. And if He lives in my heart, I will be the luckiest man, and will not need to pray for that pair of slippers, for those worldly things. I won't need to do any good deeds out of desire for Heaven or fear of Hell. My actions will be for the love of my Lord. If He is in my heart, then I will have the best of this world and the next.'"

Khalil was listening very carefully. He said, "I got it. I'm not going there to see the house of God. I'm going there to meet Him and return with Him in my heart."

Danish said "Yes, but please also remember not to break anyone's heart while you are there, because if you do that, then you shouldn't expect your prayers to be answered. People go there from all over the world. Be polite and considerate with everyone, even with people you think are not, and remember that you can't go to Heaven by pushing past others, so don't push anyone, even if it means not completing a non-obligatory ritual.

"And when you are in Medina, be respectful. You will be in the city of the Prophet ﷺ. You will be walking where the Prophet ﷺ and his companions walked. You will be praying where he and his companions prayed. You will be visiting "Paradise on Earth", as the Prophet ﷺ called it.

"But the best sign of respect would be to pledge to be obedient to the Prophet ﷺ. That is what he would love most, and it's what Allah wants us to do."

Khalil was very thankful for Danish's help. He thanked his friend, and left after saying Salam.

The lyrics of the song fueled the feelings of sorrow in Zartaj, and he started crying profusely. His tears would not stop. His uncle showed up with a friend of his, an old fellow. Zartaj could not keep himself from crying. His uncle tried to console him, but he was unable to make him feel better.

The old fellow, his uncle's friend, coughed a little and said, "Young boy, come to me next month. I may have an answer to your tears."

Zartaj was heartbroken. He said, "Old man, don't you see my pain? You can see my tears, and yet you are asking me to come next month. If you can't help me now, please don't promise me something of the future." He continued to cry.

A month passed. Zartaj had suffered a huge emotional blow, but he seemed to be picking himself up. The pain was still there, but wasn't as intense as before. He met his uncle one day and he remembered the old fellow. He asked his uncle about what the old fellow had said that day. His uncle said, "He is a wise man, so he must have something to tell you."

"But why didn't he tell me that day?" Zartaj asked.

His uncle said, "I don't know… you can ask him when you see him."

"How can I find him?" asked Zartaj.

"If you want, I can take you to his house. He is an old friend of mine, but he is not in good health these days. Why don't we go so you can ask him what he wanted to tell you? We'll also inquire after his health."

They both arrived at the old fellow's house. He was looking weak and was coughing more than before. He welcomed them both warmly and said to Zartaj, "Young boy, I was sad about how you were feeling, but what I wanted to tell you was that love is and should always be unconditional. You should not expect anything in return.

"What? Nothing in return?" asked Zartaj. "I spent my whole life becoming what she liked, and I can't expect her to at least be faithful to me?"

"Young man, her love made you what you are today, and you're still complaining? Always keep this in mind: love is unconditional and does not expect anything in return. Didn't you hear the song that day?"

"Which song?" asked Zartaj.

"The one that made you cry like a child," the old man replied.

Zartaj remembered the lyrics:

> *"I have given my heart to an uncaring beloved*
> *To the sovereign of both this world and the next"*

"Oh, it was about the love of God... You can't see Him, but you keep loving him, without expecting anything in return."

"Yes, unconditional love," said the old fellow.

"But why didn't you tell me this that day?" asked Zartaj.

"Because you were not ready. Your grief had overcome you and blinded you, and your mind was not ready to hear anything."

Zartaj understood the old man. He was now a little embarrassed. He thanked him and asked for permission to leave. The old man said, "Young man, if you come again next month, I might tell you something more."

"But why don't you tell me now?" asked Zartaj.

"No, not now. Please come next month."

Zartaj thought that the old man wasn't in good shape and might not live to next month, but he couldn't say that to him. He said goodbye and left.

Next month, Zartaj went to his uncle and asked him to go to the old fellow's place with him. His uncle said, "Oh, I'm sorry, the old fellow died a few days back. I think I forgot to tell you."

"Oh, no!" said Zartaj. "This is what I had feared. The old man promised me something that he has taken with him to the next world." Even so, he felt that he should go to the old man's house and say a prayer for his soul.

They both went to the old fellow's house, and after saying a prayer, the old fellow's son told Zartaj that his father had left a message for him. Zartaj had not expected the old fellow to fulfil his promise. The message read:

"Remember the lyrics from the song. You said it's Man talking about God, but I think... it's the other way around."

Zartaj remembered the lyrics:

> *"I have given my heart to an uncaring beloved*
> *To the sovereign of both this world and the next"*

Zartaj was surprised. "Uncaring beloved" is Man, not the God who created man and always remembers him. Who makes his heart beat every second, makes him breathe every moment. Who feeds him and protects him. It's the man who is uncaring, who forgets his Lord, his beloved.

He asked his uncle, "But how can we, Man, be the sovereign of this world and the next?"

His uncle thought for a moment and replied, "Haven't you heard these verses of Farid:

> *"If, oh beloved, you accept Farid*
> *You are the sovereign, you are the king*
> *If not, insignificant, lowly, worthless, inferior*
> *You are nothing, the nonexistent[3]"*

Notes

[1] "Crown of Gold".

[2] "*Neo La Laya*", a Punjabi Sufi song written by Shah Hussain, a 16th-century Sufi saint and poet. The song was originally sung by Hamid Ali Bela and composed by Kalay Khan. It was later sung by other singers including Kaavish in Coke Studio Pakistan.

[3] The last four verses of a Saraiki poem, "*Mendha Ishq Ve Tun*". The 19th-century Sufi poet Khawaja Ghulam Farid converses with his beloved, the Lord, in the first 42 verses, and God replies to him in these last four verses.

The Boat

The night was dark and the river was quiet. A heart-shaped boat[1] was slowly sailing towards its destination. The only available light was the light of the moon[2]. However, the moon did more than just shine; it also guided the boat's way.

The boatman[3] had set sail to visit his beloved[4], who had promised to see him. His beloved had also promised a drink[5] – a drink so pure and so refreshing that no one on Earth had ever tasted its like. A drink that could be served by his beloved and no other.

"Follow the moon," were the instructions from his beloved, "and the moon will bring you to my land.[6]" Night was dark, but the light of the moon was enough to sail by. The boatman saw shadowy figures standing on the shore in the dark, and he recognized them to be members of his family. One of the men asked, "Could you please give us some space on your boat? The night is dark, and we are stranded here." The boatman nodded and brought the boat towards them, and they all sailed off in his boat.

One of the boatman's three parrots, Amaar[7], didn't seem very happy with this kind gesture, but the boatman ignored him and moved on. After a while, a few more shadows waved at the boat, and when the boatman glided his boat over to them, he found that they were people from his hometown who also needed a ride. Amaar could no longer keep silent and cried, "Don't be foolish! There isn't enough room on the boat. You aren't here to offer a free ferry service… you're on your way to meet someone. So ignore their request and keep on moving."

Lawam[8], one of the boatman's other parrots, had kept quiet so far. He said, "Come on, you don't have to do anything out of the ordinary. These people are from your hometown and are stranded here. You should help them." The boatman brought the boat alongside them and they all boarded the boat.

The boat had become a bit heavy now and was moving slowly, but the boatman kept following the moon so he could reach his destination and meet his beloved. Once again, some shadows in the dark waved at him, and boatman discovered that they were people unfamiliar to him. They, too, were asking for a ride. Amaar was against the idea of giving them a ride, while Lawam wanted them to be accommodated. Even though these people were strangers, they were still his countryfolk. The boatman glanced at the moon and decided to let them in. His boat was a bit crowded now, but he continued to follow the moon.

A while later, a few more shadows, again unknown to the boatman, waved and asked for a ride. Amaar protested and told the boatman to not be generous toward the strangers. Lawam said that he should let the strangers on, as they were people of his faith. The boatman looked at the moon once again, and welcomed them aboard.

By this point, the boat had become very crowded. A few more shadows approached the slow-moving boat. They also asked for a ride. Amaar said, "We don't have any more space, and come on, they aren't even of your faith!"

Lawam said, "But they are still humans, stranded and in need of help."

The boatman looked at the moon and asked them to come aboard, too. Now there was hardly any room on the boat. It was really heavy and moved slowly.

The boatman saw a girl on the riverbank. She had two lambs with her and was waving at the boat. The girl asked if her lambs could be taken to a farm that was downriver. She could return to her home, but there was no space there for the lambs, and they couldn't be left out in the open. Amaar was really upset this time and said, "Now don't try to be nice to the animals!" Lawam replied that if they weren't ferried to the farm, they might be eaten by wolves in the dark. The boatman looked at the moon again, welcomed the lambs aboard, and moved on. It seemed like the boat was now overloaded and might even sink.

As they moved along, a boy waved at the boat and said to the boatman, "Sir, could you please take these fruit plants to my farm downriver? If they don't get there by morning, they could die and we'll miss the plantation for this season." Amaar couldn't bear it and cried, "Don't even think about it or you will sink!"

Lawam said, "But the boy's plants could die by morning, and then his family would suffer a huge loss." The boatman wasn't sure what to do. He looked at the moon again and decided to take the plants.

The boat was overloaded now and moved really slowly. Mutmin[9], the third parrot who had been hiding somewhere until now came out, looked at the boatman, and smiled. The boatman looked at Mutmin and was pleased to see him happy.

The boatman, in his slow, overloaded boat, kept following the moon. He was looking forward to seeing his beloved, and remembered the words of a song:

"I have found wealth in the relations
Neither does my heart bear burden, nor the slightest shadow of
sadness[10]"

All of a sudden, there were signs of an approaching storm. The boatman remembered his beloved, looked at the moon, and thought, "My destination should be close. I'll make it before the storm hits." The storm began to pick up. A huge wave took hold of the boat and to the boatman's surprise, all the passengers disappeared. The boat turned upside down. The boatman couldn't breathe. Realizing that it was over for him, he said his prayers and closed his eyes.

The boatman opened his eyes... and found himself at the doorstep of his beloved. He realized that moon had guided him to this land correctly. The way to this land was at the bottom of the river; he could have spent years and years on the surface, trying to find the way. He couldn't have reached here if he had disagreed with Lawam and had followed Amaar instead. He couldn't have made it on an empty boat. Even though it didn't seem like it when his journey began, only a full boat could have carried him to the land of his beloved.

Notes

1 Heart of Man

2 Prophet Muhammad ﷺ

3 Human being

4 God

[5] Serving the pure drink by the Lord in Heaven is mentioned in (Q76:21):

"Upon the inhabitants will be green garments of fine silk and brocade. And they will be adorned with bracelets of silver, and their Lord will give them a purifying drink."

[6] Instructions to follow the light of the Prophet ﷺ is mentioned in (Q7:157):

"Those who follow the Messenger, the unlettered prophet, whom they find written in what they have of the Torah and the Gospel, who enjoins upon them what is right and forbids them what is wrong and makes lawful for them the good things and prohibits for them the evil and relieves them of their burden and the shackles which were upon them. So they who have believed in him, honored him, supported him and followed the light which was sent down with him - it is those who will be the successful."

In the next verse (Q:7:157) it is also mentioned that:

"Say, [O Muhammad], 'O mankind, indeed I am the Messenger of Allah to you all, [from Him] to whom belongs the dominion of the heavens and the earth. There is no deity except Him; He gives life and causes death.' So believe in Allah and His Messenger, the unlettered prophet, who believes in Allah and His words, and follow him that you may be guided."

[7] *Nafs Ammara* (part of the self that encourages one to do wrong).

Mentioned in (Q12:53):

"And in no way do I acquit myself. Surely the self indeed constantly commands to odious (deeds), except that on which my Lord had mercy. Surely my Lord is Ever-forgiving, Ever-Merciful."

[8] *Nafs Lawamah* (part of the self that reproaches wrongdoings, intentions, or thoughts. Conscience). Mentioned in (Q75:2):

"And I swear by the reproaching soul [to the certainty of resurrection]."

[9] *Nafs al Mutmainna* (the self at peace). Mentioned in (Q89:27-28):

"(It will be said to the pious): 'O (you) the one in (complete) rest and satisfaction! Come back to your Lord, Well-pleased (yourself) and well-pleasing unto Him!'"

[10] From an Urdu song, *"Hansi Khanakti Hui"*. Sung by Nayyara Noor, composed by Arshad Mahmood, and written by Hassan Akber Kamal.

The Gift

Muhibbah[1] walked past the village Masjid's courtyard, where some men sat and talked. She greeted them with her charming smile and said salaam to them. They all smiled back and said salaam and prayers to the young girl.

After she left, one of the men said, "Everyone in this village loves that girl. She is the apple of everyone's eye. Everyone adores her… no other child in this village gets so much love. What do you think is the reason for that?"

One man said, "Well the reason is simple… she is an orphan. Her father died fighting for the country. Everyone considers him a hero, and that's why everyone loves her. Since he gave his life for them, they feel obligated to be nice to his daughter."

Another man interrupted and said, "No, that's not the reason! The reason is that she is very cute."

"Cute? What do you mean?" a third man interrupted.

"Well, she is cute. She has a very cute face."

"She's pretty, you mean?"

"Yes, of course! She is very pretty, and I think that's why everyone loves her."

"No, no, that's not the reason!" yet another person said. "Didn't you see her smile? It's special. It's charming, and she's always smiling. Everyone loves people who smile, especially children."

Someone else said, "No, that's not the reason! The thing is that she is very well-mannered. She speaks very politely and respectfully. Everyone loves her because she is such a well-mannered child."

Another person said, "No, that's not the reason! The reason is that she is very intelligent. She doesn't just speak well, but intelligently, too. She is very intelligent and wise for her age."

"No, that's not the reason! The reason is that she has a special gift... a God-given gift that can't be seen or explained, but can only be felt by others. And that's why everyone loves her."

"What type of gift can't be seen or explained? There must be something else," one of them said.

An old man was listening quietly. He said, "You are all partially right. The gift is actually a combination of most of these things, plus a major ingredient that you have overlooked."

"And what's that?" everyone asked.

"That is love itself. Actually, *she* is the one who loves everyone. Young or old, man or woman... everyone. She loves everyone, and she receives their love in return. That's how it goes: you love others, and others will love you."

The old man's idea seemed to have convinced everyone. Meanwhile, the Muazzin called for the Maghrib prayer, and they all left to pray.

Notes

---

[1] "The loving one"

75

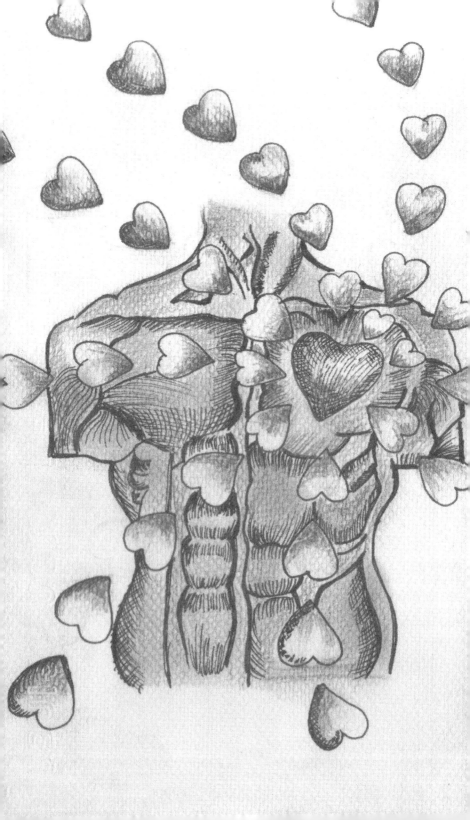

The Heart

"Surgeon, how is my heart doing now?"

"Oh, it's doing great! Doing its job almost one hundred percent now."

"Well, thanks, Surgeon. I feel like I've been given a new life. I hope it will keep doing its job properly."

"You mean pumping the blood?"

"Yes, of course! Does it have any other function?"

"Well, *biologically* it's for pumping, but…"

"But what?"

"You must have heard phrases like, 'my heart will go on', or 'don't break my heart', right?"

"Oh, yes, of course. You mean the other function… loving."

"Well, it's more than just loving. It's like a transmitter that receives and transmits love. The good thing is that there are no limits on this transmitter's frequency."

"What does that mean?"

"Well, it means that you could either limit your heart to a very low frequency, where you just love yourself and a few people around you, or you could increase its frequency to such a level that it would reach all the universes."

"So you say there are no limits on the frequency setting?"

"No, there aren't."

"But what is the use of having such a high frequency? Why would you want to have that?"

The Surgeon smiled and said, "Well, a high frequency is required to receive and send signals to the ultimate beloved, to God Himself."

"And how high a frequency would someone need to reach God?"

"As high as God is far from you."

"But God says He is closer to us than our own jugular vein![1]"

"Then that's the only frequency you'll need," the Surgeon replied.

"Surgeon, you're confusing me... first you said that I need a very high frequency, and now you're telling me that a very low frequency will do just as well!"

"If you feel God closer than your jugular vein, then you don't need to pass through galaxies, but if you don't, then you'll need to search for Him all over."

"And how will I find him?"

"By expanding your heart's frequency, by reaching the far-off skies, by letting everyone fit in your heart. By loving everyone. By ignoring the weaknesses in others and highlighting their qualities. If you do this, you won't need to look for God. He Himself will find you."

"Okay, but do I *need* to do all that?"

The Surgeon replied, "Does your heart *need* to pump?"

"Yes, of course! Without that, I'd be dead!"

"The same thing applies. Without loving, and loving unconditionally, your real heart will die. You might get a new *pumping* heart, but you can't get a new *loving* heart. That's because it's part of your soul, and your soul is immortal and irreplaceable.

"Wait, Surgeon, wait. You said that my loving heart can die, and that it's a part of my soul, but you also said that my soul *can't* die. You're confusing me!"

"Your pumping heart will die when it stops pumping and can't be revived. It won't disappear... it will still be there, just dead. If your loving heart dies and isn't revived before you die, then it's dead. Your soul remains immortal, but with a dead loving heart. I know it sounds very unpleasant, so it's better not to focus on that. Instead, focus on a healthy heart that pumps and also loves, and loves across the board."

"Surgeon, that seems even harder than heart surgery... of the pumping heart, I mean."

"Well, it's not that hard. All you need to do is to try, and remember that trying is eighty percent of doing something. So try and don't give up, because not giving up is the other twenty percent. If you follow these two simple steps, your loving heart will also work at nearly one hundred percent."

"Surgeon, one last question... why do I need to love God?"

"So that God loves you in return," the Surgeon replied.

"And how do I know if God loves me?"

"When people love you and trust you unconditionally, you'll know that God loves you. I think I should be leaving now. Goodbye, and good luck." And the Surgeon moved on.

Notes

---

[1] From (Q50:16):

"And indeed We already created man, and We know whatever his self whispers within him, and We are nearer to him than the jugular vein."

81

The King

Aina[1,2] stood in the King's[3] court and on her turn, she introduced herself and said that she loved the King very much. The King smiled and said, "Well, everyone who comes here says the same. Anyhow, what are you looking for... a house? Money?"

"No, no. Sir, I do not seek such things."

"Then what do you seek?"

"I seek nothing... but you."

Suddenly, there was pin-drop silence in the court, and everyone looked at the girl. She was a young, pretty girl with beautiful eyes, but it seemed that she couldn't see.

The King replied, "You seek me? Okay... how?"

The girl said, "I seek your love, Sir."

Everyone in the court was astonished. A man whispered, "Smart girl. She has asked for something that there is nothing above or beyond. If she is lucky and gets what she has asked for, then she'll never need anything else."

The King replied, "Young girl, you don't seem to be able to see. You have probably never seen me, and now here you are, in my court, asking for myself, for my love!"

"Yes, Sir. You're right. I seek you, I seek your love."

"Okay… and why should I love you, my dear?"

"Sir, because… I love *you*, that's why."

"But everyone claims to love me. It's easy to make such claims, but do you have any real reasons for why I should love you?"

"Well, I'll try. I seek your love because I believe in you. I believe in everyone whom you have appointed. I believe in your law, and in your judgement. I share what I have out of my love for you. I remember you every day, every morning, and every evening. I can't see you, but I always feel you very near me. You are always around me, always protecting me, always with me. I also keep the promises I make, as you have commanded, and I have remained patient in loving you… until today.[4]"

The girl had the King's attention. Everyone in the court also seemed to take interest in her now.

The King said, "Okay, and what else have you done out of your love for me?"

"Well, not only was I loyal to you, but I also fought against those who betrayed you, even though I was weak. I fought against those who were responsible for unrest and caused trouble for your people.[5]"

"Okay, that's interesting. What else did you do?"

"I have always been nice to your people. I have tried my best to give more than I receive, as it pleases you.[6]"

"Hmm… what else?"

"Even though I love you, I have always been very fearful of you. I have tried to never get involved in anything that you would not like, and if for some reason I ended up in such a situation, I regretted and repented as soon as I realized, and never did it again.[7]"

"I kept myself pure for you… pure in my heart, pure in my soul, and pure in my body.[8]"

"Hmm…"

"I always remained thankful and stayed steadfast, no matter how hard the times were, as you commanded…[9]"

"Okay, continue, I'm listening."

"I always relied on you. I did my best in any given scenario, but in the end it was the thought of you that kept me going.[10]"

"And what else did you do?"

"I remained just and fair in all matters. As fair as I could be.[11]"

The girl seemed exhausted, and had nothing more to say.

The King smiled, stood up, walked up to the girl, presented her with a purifying drink, and said, "There is no doubt that you deserve all my love. This is what I promised, and here do I fulfill it."

Notes

[1] Human

[2] "Beautiful-eyed woman"

[3] God

[4] Aina is claiming to be righteous in her first reason to the King.

God mentions in Quran that He loves "*Mutaqeen*" (the righteous). It is mentioned in (Q3:76):

> "Yes indeed, (but) whoever fulfils his covenant and is righteous (to Allah), then surely Allah loves the righteous."

and in (Q9:7):

> "How can there be for the polytheists a treaty in the sight of Allah and with His Messenger, except for those with whom you made a treaty at al-Masjid al-Haram? So as long as they are upright toward you, be upright toward them. Indeed, Allah loves the righteous [who fear Him]."

Then in (Q2:177), God explains who the righteous are:

> "Righteousness is not that you turn your faces toward the east or the west, but [true] righteousness is [in] one who believes in Allah , the Last Day, the angels, the Book, and the prophets and gives wealth, in spite of love for it, to relatives, orphans, the needy, the traveller, those who ask [for help], and for freeing slaves; [and who] establishes prayer and gives zakat; [those who] fulfill their promise when they promise; and [those who] are patient in poverty and hardship and during battle. Those are the ones who have been true, and it is those who are the righteous."

[5] In her second reason, she claims to be a fighter. God mentioned in Quran that He loves "*Yukatiloon*" (fighters) in (Q61:4):

"Indeed, Allah loves those who fight in His cause in a row as though they are a [single] structure joined firmly."

[6] In her third reason, she claims to be a doer of good. God mentions that He loves "*Muhsineen*" (doers of good) in (Q3:134):

"Who spend [in the cause of Allah] during ease and hardship and who restrain anger and who pardon the people - and Allah loves the doers of good"

[7] In her fourth reason, Aina claims to be repentant. God mentions that He loves "*Tawabeen*" (repentant ones) in (Q2:222).

"And they ask you about menstruation. Say, "It is harm, so keep away from wives during menstruation. And do not approach them until they are pure. And when they have purified themselves, then come to them from where Allah has ordained for you. Indeed, Allah loves those who are constantly repentant and loves those who purify themselves."

[8] In her fifth reason, she claims to be the purified one. God also mentions that He loves "*Mutahireen*" (those who purify themselves) in (Q2:222).

God also mentions His love of "*Mutahireen*" (those who purify themselves) in (Q9:108):

"Do not stand [for prayer] within it - ever. A mosque founded on righteousness from the first day is more worthy for you to stand in. Within it are men who love to purify themselves; and Allah loves those who purify themselves."

[9] In her sixth reason, Aina claims to be the steadfast one. God mentions that He loves "*Sabiroon*" (the steadfast) in (Q3:146):

"And how many a prophet [fought and] with him fought many religious scholars. But they never lost assurance due to what afflicted them in the cause of Allah, nor did they weaken or submit. And Allah loves the steadfast."

[10] In her seventh reason, Aina claimed that she is the one who relies on the King (God). God mentions that He loves *"Mutawalkaleen"* (those who rely on Him) in (Q3:159):

> *"So by mercy from Allah, [O Muhammad], you were lenient with them. And if you had been rude [in speech] and harsh in heart, they would have disbanded from about you. So pardon them and ask forgiveness for them and consult them in the matter. And when you have decided, then rely upon Allah. Indeed, Allah loves those who rely [upon Him]."*

[11] In her eighth and final reason, she claims to be just and fair. God mentions that He loves *"Muksateen"* (those who act justly) in (Q49:9):

> *"And if two factions among the believers should fight, then make settlement between the two. But if one of them oppresses the other, then fight against the one that oppresses until it returns to the ordinance of Allah. And if it returns, then make settlement between them in justice and act justly. Indeed, Allah loves those who act justly."*

Spiritual Guide

"Arif[1], I have finally met your spiritual guide. Sorry, no offence, but I am a bit confused. He doesn't look like a spiritual guide at all! He was clean-shaven, wore Western clothing, and didn't look spiritual at all. I wonder what you see in him…"

"Well, you don't have to look like a spiritual guide to be one, and people who look that way might actually not be very spiritual," Arif replied.

"But what did you see in him?" asked Faisal.

"Well, I have learned valuable principles from him."

"I thought you're supposed to learn something more than just principles from a 'spiritual leader'."

"Yes, we all think so. But in life you need to learn principles, and not just learn them, but you should also witness someone applying those principles in his own life. Sermons are easy to give, but a living example is not easy to find. And if you *do* find someone, you should learn from him. He becomes your spiritual leader. It's that simple."

"So, what did you learn from him?"

"Okay, let's go in reverse. What questions will we be asked on the Day of Judgement?"

"The first one will be about prayer, *Salat*.[2]"

"Okay, right. And then?"

"Well, I think I've forgotten."

"Okay, let me tell you. No person will pass onward without answering these five questions:

1.   How did you live your life on Earth?
2.   How did you utilize your youth?
3.   How did you earn your wealth?
4.   How did you spend it?
5.   What did you do with your knowledge?[3]

"I need to see a person with my own eyes who has lived an exemplary life, who has had a spotless and productive youth, who has earned all of his wealth lawfully and spent it wisely, and has spread his knowledge not by giving sermons, but as a living example. If that person is clean-shaven and wears Western clothing, I won't mind."

Notes

¹ "The one knowing the truth"

² Refers to the following Hadith (saying of Prophet Muhammad ﷺ):

> *"The first thing among their deeds for which the people will be brought to account on the Day of Resurrection will be prayer. Our Lord will say to His angels, although He knows best, 'Look at My slave's prayer, is it complete or lacking?' If it is complete, it will be recorded as complete, but if it is lacking, He will say, 'Look and see whether my slave did any voluntary (nafil) prayers.' If he had done voluntary prayers, He will say, 'Complete the obligatory prayers of My slave from his voluntary prayers.' Then the rest of his deeds will be examined in a similar manner." (Abu Dawood)*

³ Refers to the following Hadith:

> *"The son of Adam will not pass away from Allah until he is asked about five things: how he lived his life, and how he utilized his youth, with what means did he earn his wealth, how did he spend his wealth, and what did he do with his knowledge."*
> *(Tirmidhi)*

The Hut

It was a horrible winter last year. No one had seen that much snow in years. It was really hard to even walk, as everything was covered with snow, but my hut was really comfortable inside. My fireplace was a blessing. All I needed was dry wood, which luckily I had collected when the weather was fair. It was quite cozy inside even when it was freezing outside, when the sun hadn't shown up for many days.

Even this summer was unusual. I don't know whether it was climate change or what, but the mercury really shot up this summer. There was a severe heat wave… unusual for this area. But luckily, again my small hut was really comfortable inside. The thick walls helped stop the heat from penetrating inside. The orientation of my hut also prevented direct sunlight from hitting the main living area, especially the windows. It was really comfortable inside through the whole summer.

This year, there were also unexpected flash showers, and a couple actually lasted a few days. Luckily, my hut's roof was strong, and didn't leak. My hut was all dry on the inside, safe and comfortable. To have a strong, safe, and comfortable hut really is a blessing. It should be strong enough to weather all conditions, and must be maintained continuously, otherwise it won't be able to give shelter through all these storms, both usual and unusual.

The guy who helps me do the maintenance work is an old fellow, but he's really handy. He knows almost all the trades, and helps with all the maintenance work I need. I asked him once, since he's quite old, how long he planned on working till. He replied that he's really proud of making his own living, and wouldn't mind working as long as his health allows him to. I asked him whether he had a retirement plan for when, one day, his health might not allow him to work any longer. He smiled and said, "I think I've saved up a little."

After the harsh weather this year, I tried to find the old fellow, but I was told that he was sick. I asked where he lived and planned to visit him to inquire after his well-being. When I went to his house, I was surprised to see that even though the guy himself was a tradesman, he lived in a very small, simple house, and had very little, very basic furniture inside.

The old man was lying on a simple bed. He was glad to see me. After asking how he was feeling, I asked, "You seem to be in a poor state... what about your retirement plan?"

He replied, "It's there, but it isn't time to use that yet."

The old man was sick and seemed to be in pain, but he was smiling. I asked him how he still had a smile on his face in such sickness. He said that he was safe and comfortable inside, just as

I felt safe and comfortable in my hut. I asked how he could feel safe and comfortable inside. He told me that his faith is like a hut that his soul lives in, and is very safe, comfortable, and at peace. I asked him, "Do you need to do maintenance on your hut?"

He said, "Yes, just as you need to maintain yours. Without maintenance, the hut would be in poor shape, and wouldn't be able to hold my soul in peace."

I asked whether his hut also experienced storms and rough weather. He replied, "Yes, of course it does! And that's why maintenance is very important. I need to keep my hut, my faith, in really good shape, otherwise my soul wouldn't be happy, and you might not see this smile on my face."

I asked, "You have lived a very active life. Don't you get bored lying down and doing nothing?"

He smiled and said, "While it seems like I'm doing nothing, I try to do something productive."

"And what is that?" I asked.

He said, "I pray. I pray for my family who is not here anymore. I pray for myself, and I pray for all the people I know."

"How is that productive?" I asked.

"Well, it strengthens my hut, and I feel good about all the people I pray for. After I die, I will probably be seeing the people who are not around, and hopefully they will be glad that I remembered them in this world."

Before leaving, I asked one final question. "Aren't you afraid of death?"

He replied, "If you have a strong, solid hut, you don't fear anything. Fear does not exist anymore. Even death cannot scare you."

A few days passed, and I heard that the old man had died. I thought the poor man didn't get a chance to use his retirement plan. I went to his funeral, and was surprised to see a lot more people than I expected at the funeral of such a simple man. I met an old lady and asked, "Was he a close relative?"

She told me that he wasn't. Her deceased husband was a friend of his, and after his death, the old man had helped her raise her family. She said that now all her children were grown up, educated, and well-settled. I looked around and I saw so many faces, which all seemed to be part of the old man's retirement plan. I realized that he was much smarter than I thought, and must be enjoying his infinite retirement plan up above.

Living in the Moment

"Grandfather, you say that one should live in the moment, free from any regrets of the past or worries of the future. Well, regrets of the past, that part I can understand, but how can one live without any worries of the future, especially when you have to plan things in advance, whether it's education, career, business, or anything else?

"I think your theory has some error. All successful people have lived in the future. They did things ahead of their time, which made them successful. All research and development is done in advance. Scientists and inventors virtually live in the future to develop the latest inventions. Doctors, scientists, businessmen, they all live in the future to do something new, something productive.

"Every business plans things in advance to stay ahead of the competition. Industry, technology… it's all based on the future. There wouldn't be any development if all these leaders weren't ahead of their time. It's not about living in the future… it's about *creating* the future. Taking your destiny into your own hands. A person chilling out or living in the moment can and will not be able to create the future.

"So living the moment seems like a very old-fashioned theory that leads to stagnation, not development. For me, it's like just being chill, with no regrets of the past and no worries of the future... a 'Hakuna Matata'-type life."

"Grandson, all the people you mentioned are achievers. Most achievers are passionate about what they do. Passion is love. They love what they do. When they do what they love, they are the ones who are living in the moment, not the ones who are 'chilling out'. All they need to do is to maintain a balance between their spiritual, physical, family, and professional life. If they sacrifice one for the other, there will be imbalance in their life, which will not let them live every moment. A person who is really busy in his career but isn't spending enough valuable time with his family will have imbalance in his life. Another person who pays no attention to his physical health and doesn't take care of his body will have imbalance in his life, and will not be able to live every moment. Another person who is spiritually dissatisfied, not connected to the oneness of the universe and not fueled by the divine force will also not be able to live every moment. 'Hakuna Matata'-type people are not living in the moment. Their eyes have been covered, and they are trying to live a virtual life. Actually they are the ones who are doing the opposite: instead of living in the moment, every real moment of their life is passing by or being wasted.

"Creating the future... well, there are controllable factors we can work on, and then there are uncontrollable factors. We can and must do our part working on the controllable factors, and enjoy doing it, but we should not worry about the uncontrollable factors. A farmer can prepare the best soil, sow the best seed, provide the best fertilizer, and water his fields well, but he can't control the weather, storms, or unknown diseases. So after doing his part, he shouldn't worry about the uncontrollables. If he has done his job well, regardless of the outcome, he won't have any regrets and shouldn't have any worries for the future.

"Successful people enjoy the journeys they embark on, irrespective of whether they reach their destination or not. They are more at peace during their journey than they are upon reaching their destination, and if they reach their destination, they set off on another journey so they can continue to enjoy living every moment."

The Walnut Tree

Tawaab[1], a young man, was walking down a dirt path, which passed through his little village and onward to the nearby town. He noticed a small plant on the side of the trail, and he felt like pulling it out. He approached the plant and was about to pluck it when suddenly, a farmer shouted at him from nearby, "Don't pluck it! It's a tree sapling."

Tawaab looked at the plant and thought, "It's just a small sapling," and then he went ahead and plucked it out. The farmer seemed quite upset, but didn't say anything and turned back to his work.

Tawaab felt a little embarrassed, but continued his walk along the trail. He felt guilt in his heart that it hadn't been much fun to pluck that sapling, and that he hadn't listened to the farmer, even though he had warned him. But he tried to console himself and said, "It was just a little sapling anyway, and there must be a lot more out there, so it isn't a big deal." In the meantime he saw a jeep passing by, travelling in the opposite direction. It was very rare to have any traffic on this trail. He thought it might be some government official visiting the area, and continued on his journey. After walking for about half an hour, he met a young man from a nearby village whom he had heard a bit about. It was said that he didn't have a good reputation, and spent most of his time in the town. After exchanging initial greetings, they chatted for a while. The young man mentioned that he was also going into town, and so Tawaab accompanied him.

* * * * *

Fifty years passed since then. Tawaab was now old and weak, and was lying on his bed. He didn't know why he had just remembered plucking that tree sapling, but for some reason, he really regretted it. Why? He didn't know… it was just a tree sapling, just a small one. He tried to recall what had happened afterwards.

After plucking the sapling, he had kept on going, had passed that jeep, then he had met that guy from the other village. They had become friends, close friends. That guy didn't have a good reputation, and rightly so. In an unpleasant event that Tawaab had had nothing to do with, that guy had falsely blamed him, which had resulted in a bad reputation for him as well.

"Oh, that reputation, even though I wasn't involved! That reputation had ruined everything! It ruined my chances of getting married to the girl I liked. I was unhappy, depressed. It affected my career, and I continued to struggle with it for the rest of my life. My personal life was also miserable throughout. And now here I am, old, weak, and full of regrets. I wish I had had a different life, a better one, with a better career, a better personal life!"

He remembered plucking that tree sapling once again, and again the feeling of regret came over him. He thought that he should never have done that. He prayed to God to forgive him of all his wrongdoings, and for plucking that tree sapling. He felt tired and closed his eyes.

He opened his eyes and was surprised to see the farmer who warned him against plucking the tree sapling sitting next to him. He recognized him right away and said, "How amazing it is that I was thinking about the incident in which we first met! You haven't changed much in all these years. Anyway, how are you? Good to see you... actually, it's good to see anyone, since I'm quite lonely, sick, and old."

The farmer smiled and said, "Good to see you, too."

Tawaab said, "Well, I'm sorry. I really can't offer you anything, since I can hardly get out of bed. Oh, I wish I had a different life!"

"You *could* have had one," the farmer replied.

"What? What did you say?" asked Tawaab.

"You *could* have had an altogether very different life if..."

"If *what?*" Tawaab was very curious now.

"If you had not plucked that tree sapling."

"What? That small tree sapling? How could my life have been different by not plucking it?"

"Well, it would be very different... perhaps something like this:

"You were going to pluck that tree sapling. I saw you and shouted at you, and asked you not to do it. You stopped and asked me what kind of sapling it was. I told you that it was a walnut tree sapling. You thanked me for warning you. I offered you water to drink, since it was quite hot that day. You accepted, and then I brought you some water. We chatted for a while, and in the meantime, a jeep approached us. A man got out and asked for water. He was a government official from the Department of Education. He was supposed to visit the schools in the area. He asked if you could show him the way to the schools. You accepted, and went with him."

"So I never went to the town, and never met that guy from the other village, and never became his friend!"

"Yes, that's right.

"The official was thankful for your help. He told you about a government scholarship plan for young people from rural areas. You applied for it and were accepted. You received the best education for free.

"After completing your education, you visited your village. You came to see me. You were about to go back to your home when it started to rain really hard. You took shelter under the walnut tree right there, where we had met for the first time... the same walnut tree that was a sapling a few years before. You were surprised to discover that the girl you liked, along with her father, had also taken shelter under the same tree.

"You chatted with the girl's father, rather trying to impress him with your achievements. You later helped them reach their home safely. The father also offered you a cup of tea, and you accepted. You managed to win her father's heart, and got married to the girl you liked."

"And I had a happy life thereafter, both personal and professional."

"Yes, you did."

"I wish I had had that life. I wish I... I... had never plucked that tree sapling." He felt sad and weak. He closed his eyes.

Tawaab opened his eyes, looked around, and got up. He was in his house in his village, young and full of energy. He thought, "Oh, that must have been a dream! What a horrible dream it had been." He then thought, "Oh, yes! I had planned to visit the city. Nothing special. I might see a friend or two there. I've just become bored, staying in the village after my exams."

He took a shower, changed, and then set off on a walk into town. He had almost forgotten his dream, and walked with his mind filled with thoughts of the town. Suddenly, he saw a small plant on the side of the track, and felt like pulling it out. A feeling of déjà vu came over him. He approached the plant, and saw that it was a tree sapling. It was then that he remembered the dream. He looked around and saw that there was no farmer around. He knew he shouldn't even touch the sapling. He waited for the farmer to appear, but he was nowhere to be found. Then he thought of the jeep, he looked along the track, but there was no sign of any jeep. He waited and waited, but neither farmer nor jeep arrived.

Then he thought that the dream must be false. "I shouldn't believe in dreams. Not all dreams are supposed to be true. Why shouldn't I just pluck the sapling and move on?" He was about to pluck the sapling, but then he thought, "Whether or not the dream is true, I should always be doing what is right, no matter how small it seems." He felt that pulling that sapling out was not right.

He dropped the idea of plucking the sapling, felt good in his heart, and kept on moving.

Notes

---

[1] "The one who repents"

The Witch

The jungle was dark and deep. Zahid[1] was travelling alone. This jungle had long been known as a hiding place for witches. They had been banished from the city long ago because of their sins, cruelty, and cannibalism. Before being thrown out into the woods, the leader of the witches, an old hag, had negotiated with the city's elders to be allowed to continue their hunt in the woods, on the condition that they would only hunt men who willingly walked all the way to their hideout. However, they would be free to exploit any of their prey's weaknesses in order to make them do so.

Zahid was a pious man. He fulfilled all his obligations, loved his family, and considered himself to be a good man who had hardly any weaknesses. He knew that the jungle was the home of the accursed witches, but he still decided to travel through it. He thought that since he had no apparent weaknesses, he wouldn't be harmed by them.

He reached the middle of the jungle. It was scarier than he had thought it would be, but his confidence that he was a man without any weaknesses kept him going.

The old witch noticed someone travelling through the jungle, and ordered her most beautiful witch to go to the traveller, lure him with her beauty, and bring him to their hideout.

The beautiful witch got ready and left to snare her prey. She made her way to a path where Zahid was expected to pass and hid behind a tree. She laid down with her back against the tree trunk. She leaned her head to one side as if she were fast asleep. As she laid down, she noticed that Zahid was approaching. She moved her wrist, and her bangles made a very attractive sound in the dark jungle.

Zahid heard the sound, and at first he got scared. He thought of the witches, but then he thought, why would a witch be wearing bangles? Maybe there was a lady stranded in the jungle. Or it might just be his imagination. He decided to explore further, and moved in the direction of the sound. Behind the tree, he found a young, beautiful lady lying against a tree. Zahid was mesmerized by her beauty, and for a moment he forgot all about the witches.

He was about to wake her up when he once again suspected that she might be a witch. "But how could she be a witch?" thought Zahid. "She is so beautiful, young and innocent. Witches are probably old, ugly, and scary. But if she is human, why is she lying here in this jungle at night? I should wake her up and ask."

Once again, he was just about to wake her up, but then the thought of his family entered his mind. He remembered his wife, who was waiting for him at home. "Witch or not," he thought, "I should move on. This lady is none of my business."

Zahid moved on. The witch was surprised by his behaviour. She stood up and went back to her hideout. The old witch had been monitoring the whole situation from there. She said to the pretty witch, "It's okay my dear, don't you worry. This traveller has no weakness for beauty, but never mind… we will try something else."

She asked another witch to take up the hunt. This witch was fair-looking, but had a very sweet voice. She spoke so beautifully, it seemed that she is talking in poetry. She got all ready, and left for her prey. She also hid behind a tree on the path Zahid was expected to follow. As Zahid approached, she moved her wrist, and her bangles made a beautiful sound in the dark jungle.

Zahid heard the sound and stopped. He moved towards the tree from where the sound had come. He saw a young, fair-looking lady standing behind the tree. He was a little cautious this time and asked who she was. The young lady replied, "Oh, I am Laila… who are you, handsome?"

The unexpected compliment made Zahid blush, and couldn't help but introduce himself. Laila listened to him attentively and replied, "Oh, I live in a nearby village and entered the jungle to collect some firewood, and then I realized that I had lost my anklet. I was trying to find it… but now I have found you." She spoke in such a beautiful way, in such a sweet voice, that Zahid wanted to listen to her all night.

But all of a sudden he remembered the witches and asked Laila, "But isn't this place known to have witches?" Laila replied, "Come on, you're so handsome and yet you still believe in those fairy tales? I live here, and no one in our village has ever seen anything like that. Those are all just rumours." Zahid could argue no further. Laila said, "I think I could find my anklet if a young and handsome man like you were helping me."

"What if I don't?" asked Zahid.

"Well, I'd still have a wonderful time in your company."

Zahid was almost overwhelmed by her sweet voice, poetic speech, and compliment after compliment, but then he remembered that it was a long way home, that his wife is waiting for him there, and that he had no business with this young lady. He excused himself to Laila and moved on.

Laila was surprised and upset, and when she returned to her hideout, the old witch said to her, "Oh, we have not seen anyone like this stranger in years, who has weakness for neither beauty nor flattery. Don't you worry, girls… let me handle him." She put on a gorgeous dress, and covered her head so her face hardly showed; it was hard to tell if she was old or young, especially in the dark. She took a sip of hot water to soften her voice, and went out in search of her prey.

She found the path Zahid was on and hid behind a tree. As Zahid approached, she started to cry softly. Zahid heard the voice and stopped. He came to that tree and found a lady who wore a beautiful dress, had her head covered, and was crying.

He had already met two women, or witches… whoever they were. And even if they were witches, they couldn't harm him anyway, since he was perfect and free of all weakness. His confidence in himself was greater than ever. He bravely asked the lady, "Who are you, and why are you crying?"

The witch answered softly, "Oh, I am a traveller like you."

"What are you doing in this dark jungle at such a late hour?" asked Zahid.

"Actually, I was travelling with a man who claimed that he loved me but…" She started crying again. "But he was a fraud. He cheated me. He made false promises. Asked me to run away from my family, and to bring all my jewelry, and said that he would marry me. But he left me in this deep, dark jungle and ran away with all my valuables." She burst into tears once more.

Zahid's heart was moved. The heart that had not been touched by beauty or flattery had been moved by the tears of this witch. She continued:

"I cannot go back to my home. My family will not accept me. I am all ruined!" said the witch.

117

"Oh, don't you worry, poor lady. There must be some way. Don't you think yourself alone. Perhaps God has sent me to help you," said Zahid.

"Oh, I felt like I was going to die in this darkness! Could you please help me find the man who took all my jewelry? He couldn't have gone far, and he went in *that* direction."

The witch pointed.

Zahid was all caught up in her tears. His brain had stopped thinking. He thought of neither his home nor his wife, and started walking in the direction the witch had pointed in, filled with the feeling that he was being helpful. Little did he know that he was walking toward the witches' den, where he would soon be eaten alive.

Notes

1 "The pious one"

God Wants You to Be a Superman

"Mirror, mirror, what does God want me to be? I have always had this question in my mind. I always knew that He wanted me to be something, but what, *that* I don't know. He did not want me to be a monk living in a cave. He did not want me to be a worshipper who stayed in a *masjid*. He did not want me to be a person who is totally lost in the affairs of this world, whose life revolves around material things. Then what does He want?"

The mirror replied, "God wants you to be… a superman."

"What? A superman?"

"Yes, a superman. He wants you to rise above your selfish needs. Rise above laying back and waiting for things to happen. To be proactive. To take control."

"What should I control?" I asked the mirror.

"The controllables. You can control your needs, your greed, your anger, and your laziness."

"But I can't control the uncontrollables... the weather, for example."

"No, you cannot. Haven't you heard the prayer that says, 'Lord, give me the courage to change the things that can and ought to be changed, the serenity to accept the things that cannot be changed, and the wisdom to know the difference'?

"God wants you to have faith... not just faith in Him, but faith in yourself, too. Haven't you heard that knowing yourself leads to knowing God? God wants you to have principles, not goals."

"What, no goals? I've always heard people talking about the importance of setting and meeting goals."

"Yes, you must have, but if you have strong principles, and if you follow them, then you will not need to set goals. A goal is limited, whereas principles will take you to the land of the unlimited. To the land of God, who is unlimited. There, you won't even know it, and all your 'goals' will be met. Change yourself, and the world will be changed, because you are the tiny pupil of an eye – small though it may be, but it can capture the entire horizon.

"God wants you to take control of yourself. Be disciplined, because discipline leads to freedom. God wants you to stick to the right principles. Keep doing what's right, no matter what the situation is. It might sound hard in the beginning, but then you will be fueled by divine powers, which will remove your fears.

And once the fear of failure is removed from your heart, you will be free. You will be a superman, who will live an immortal life, not afraid of death because it will only be a transition from one world into another, just like the transition that occurs when a person leaves the womb of his mother and comes to this world. His tiny world of the womb was his comfort zone, but then he is forced to move out, and enters this world. And then this world becomes his comfort zone, and he wants to never leave it. But everyone has to go to another, much bigger world. So it will be a transition. But in the meantime, God does not want you to wish for this transition to take place sooner."

"If it's a bigger, much better world (only if I do things right, of course), why wouldn't He?"

"He wants you to always remember that the transition will be inevitable, and that it could come at any time. You should always be prepared for it, but He does not want you to wish for it."

"Well, that's tricky."

"Yes, it is, but the reason He doesn't want you to wish for it is because He wants you to be successful in this world. He wants you to be a leader here, not a person simply waiting for the transition. He wants you to be a man of both worlds. Like a racer who is running and sweating. He may be tired at times, but he enjoys his race. He knows that the race will come to an end soon, but he does not wish for the race to end and be rewarded for his effort. This is only possible when he is actually enjoying his run."

"How do I enjoy the run? Life, I mean."

"Well, there are some illusions of happiness that are actually not happiness."

"Like what?"

"Material things like clothing, jewelry, gadgets. They create a false illusion of happiness for a very short while, but actually they don't give people real happiness."

"Then how? By giving all these things up?"

"No, not by giving these things up. God wants you to have balance in your life. Happiness does not come if you pray all night, either. Happiness comes from helping others, by being with others, and by sharing, even if it's only a smile. It comes from giving, superman. Haven't you heard? 'With great power comes great responsibility.'"

"But that was in Spiderman," I corrected.

"Whatever," the mirror said, and then it spoke no more.

About the Author

Zain Hashmi was born in Lahore, Pakistan in 1976. In his early years, he lived in various cities in Pakistan, and in Jeddah, Saudi Arabia. Having also lived in Toronto, Canada he has experienced life in both the East and West. He is an MBA by education, and runs a consulting firm.

Zain Hashmi is from a family of Sufi saints. He is named after his great grandfather, the last Sufi saint in his lineage, who died in 1942. He is a descendant of Baha-ud-Din Zakariya, a prominent 13th-century Sufi saint of the sub-continent who belonged to the clan of the Prophet Muhammad ﷺ, Banu Hashim.

Made in United States
Troutdale, OR
02/26/2024

17980230R00087